Weeds and Wild Flowers

Weeds and Wild Flowers

Poems by Alice Oswald

Etchings by Jessica Greenman

faber and faber

First published in 2009
by Faber and Faber Ltd
Bloomsbury House, 74–77 Great Russell Street
London WC1B 3DA

Typeset in Janson by Faber and Faber Limited
Printed in England by
T. J. International Ltd, Padstow, Cornwall

A CIP record for this book
is available from the British Library

ISBN 978–0–571–23749–4

2 4 6 8 10 9 7 5 3

The map of spring must be forever redrawn.

AIMÉ CÉSAIRE

Weeds and Wild Flowers, which grew out of a number of conversations with Jessica Greenman, is not an illustrated book. It is two separate books, a book of etchings and a book of poems, shuffled together. What connects them both is their contention that flowers are recognisably ourselves elsewhere; but whereas the etchings express that thought dynamically in the postures of the pictures, the poems make fun of it, using the names of flowers to summon up the flora of the psyche. My hope is that the experience of reading and looking at the book will be a slightly unsettling pleasure, like walking through a garden at night, when the plants come right up to the edges of their names and then beyond them. It is not, for that reason, a reliable guide to wild flowers, though it may be a reliable record of someone's wild or wayside selves.

ALICE OSWALD

It's difficult to say whether my response to flowers or the process of etching itself is the more profound. Etching requires immersion in acid, called 'biting', to produce a plate from which the prints are taken and the original drawing is reversed; the negative becomes positive. The flowers themselves act on my mind in a way that reminds me of being similarly submerged; they bite into me. There is always a terrible worry about foul biting, which is when you have failed to de-grease the plate properly and the acid crawls under the bitumen surface which has been smoked in flame, and eats it away. A whole plate can be destroyed, and that happened in fact with a pansy print that cannot be featured here. The etching I do involves engulfment in a powerful external force (nature, acid) for a long time: I can stare at a flower for weeks, and the ferric chloride takes many hours to work on the metal. What then emerges is a very precisely corroded line that contains everything I've been looking at; the culmination of what has been absorbed. The mirror-image aspect has some relevance to my relationship with Alice and her poems; varied but exact.

JESSICA GREENMAN

Weeds and Wild Flowers

Jessica Greenman September 2006

Stinking Goose-foot

Stinking Goose-foot has grown human.
It could happen to anyone.

Has no bath.
Keeps his socks in a bag
that he hangs on a nail by the door.

And his wife in the earth.

In the wet season, in the wasteground,
poking around with a spade, you'll see him
put slugs in a bag.
Which he pops in his mouth.

Or at puddles he stands
soaping his hands, but his breath
smells lonesome
his toes are decayed underneath.

He loves sitting up late,
eating sweet biscuits,
unbinding a bandaged foot
which scrunches and itches.

And the little mealy lines of his veins
show what a trouble it's been
to be quite this strange.

How it stretches his neck
to peer here and there as he goes
slowly along the back lanes
when apparently he's got webbed toes.

All he knows is his hands,
when he creeps and leans on his cane,
seem as old as the lanes
but as strong as good twine.

Daisy

I will not meet that quiet child
roughly my age but match-size
I will not kneel low enough to her lashes
to look her in her open eye
or feel her hairy wiry strength
or open my mouth among her choristers
I will not lie small enough under her halo
to smell its laundered frills
or let the slightest whisperiness
find out her friendliness
because she is more
summer-like more meek
than I am I will push my nail
into her neck and make
a lovely necklace out of her green bones

Jessica Greenman 12th–18th June 2003

Jessica Greenman June 30th–July 3rd 2000

Jessica Greenman July 10th–17th 2000

Bristly Ox-tongue

It is Bristly Ox-tongue,
too shy to speak.
Long silence.
It is Bristly Ox-tongue.

Who stands rooted
with his white hair uncombed.
Long silence.
He stands rooted.

He stands rooted
with his white hair uncombed,
pulling it out in handfuls.
This is no good.

Long silence.
He carries this silence everywhere,
like an implement from long ago,
he carries it everywhere.

This is Bristly Ox-tongue.
Long silence.
He has enormous jaws, chewing on silence.
He has enormous jaws, chewing on silence.

This is no good.
He has come indoors in his boots
and anyhow, his hands are more like hooves.
This is no good.

If only he was among his own kind,
rutting and feeding by night, hiding by day.
Long silence.
I said if only he was among his own kind.

If only he was among his own kind
standing in groups by the roadside
or making small clumps on the cliffs.
Now that would be good.

May 5th 2008
Jessica Greenman

Bastard Toadflax

Ponderous, obstinate,
cold-skinned person.
Very swollen eyes.
Gets fidgets often.

Makes passes
at unsuspecting lasses.
Tips chair, untips chair.

Tips. Untips.
Sits in damp places
flattering and heckling.

Pushes pudge of tongue-tip
into bulge of lower lip.

Loves tickling.

Gets terrible itches.
Tries used-up matches in his ears.
Keeps young girl waiting while he scratches.

Full of blotches.
Wide-mouthed, winking.
Has monstrous appetites.
Is always drinking.

Many a helpless motherly lass
smoothes down her dress,

cooks quantities of porridge.
And mentions marriage.

Marriage?

Extreme headache
slides over one eyebrow.

Only swearing can help now.

THE TALE OF SAMUEL WHISKERS

THE TALE OF SAMUEL WHISKERS OR The Roly Poly Pudding

by BEATRIX POTTER

"F. WARNE & Co"

THE GREEN FAIRY BOOK

ANDREW LANG

LONGMANS & Co

Jessica Greenman April 21st ~ 23rd 2003

Violet

Recently fallen, still with wings out,
she spoke her name to summon us to her darkness.

Not wanting to be seen, but not uncurious,
she spoke her name and let her purple deep eye-pupil
                                        be peered into.

'Violet,' she said
and showed her heart under its leaf.

Then she leant a little frightened forwards
and picked a hand to pick her.

And her horrified mouseface, sniffed and lifted close,
let its gloom be taken and all the sugar licked off its strangeness

while we all stood there saying, 'Violet! Violet!'
fingering her blue bruised skin.

Finally she mentioned
the name of her name

which was something so pin-sharp,
in such a last gasp of a previously unknown language,

it could only be spoken as a scent,
it could only be heard as our amazement.

Jessica Greenman April 98

To see a World in a Grain of Sand
And a Heaven' in a Wild Flower,
Hold Infinity in the palm of your hand
And eternity in an hour.

William Blake, Auguries of Innocence

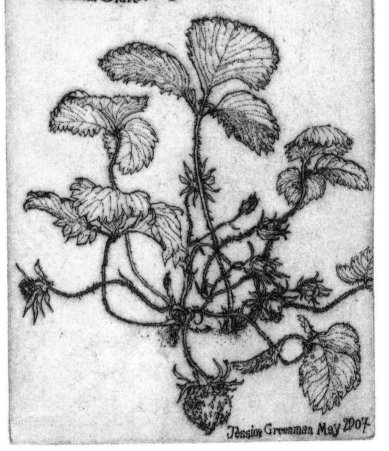

Jessica Greenman May 2007

Thrift

Born by the sea.
Used to its no-hope moan.
Forty or thereabouts.
Lived on her own.

Heaved a small sigh.
With a handful of stone
to get started,
she saved up the rain.

She came with her cushion
to the cliffs. She sat
strained in the wind
in a pink old-fashioned hat.

No prospect
but the plunge of the beach.
All except nodding,
no speech.

But she worked she worked
to the factory rhythm
of the sea's boredom.
Its bouts of atheism.

And by the weekend
set up a stall
of paper flowers.
And sold them all.

So she made substance out of
lack of substance.
Hard of hearing,
she thrived on silence.

Bargeman's Cabbage

Bargeman himself
Has a large hard head.
All day and night
Mostly he thinks of heaviness.
His stoop is rusted up
From pushing and hoisting.
And that's OK
That's all good business.

But Bargeman's Cabbage
She has her bare brown toes.
She has her cleavage.
She holds herself compact and cool.
All day and night
Mostly she paints the buckets.
She puts her feet up on the rail.
She can't be budged.
No, she's not coal.

Bargeman himself
Is murky, slow-spoken.
He does the slops.
He mops the kitchen.
His mouth is all mushed in
From saying nothing.
And that's OK
That's his profession.

But Bargeman's Cabbage,
No, she's not haulage.
All day and night
She paints black flowers.
She clips her nails –
A little fleet of trimmings in the canal.
She gets depressed by mud-banks.
But won't be put ashore. No, she's not planks.

She smells of blight.
It's in her clothes.
Won't be long now.
Her hands are very white.
She sits up late.
Her heart is damp
And tightly closed.
She leans as if she's listening but
Who knows?

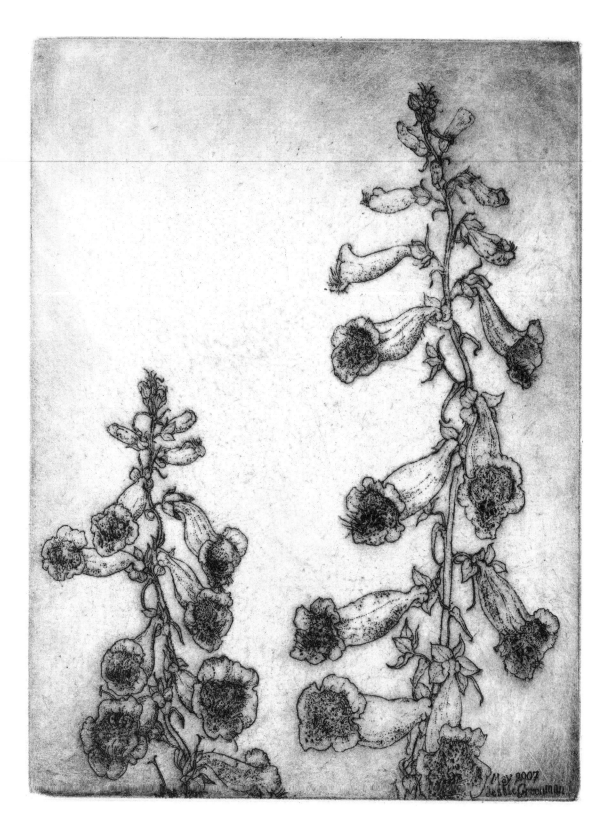

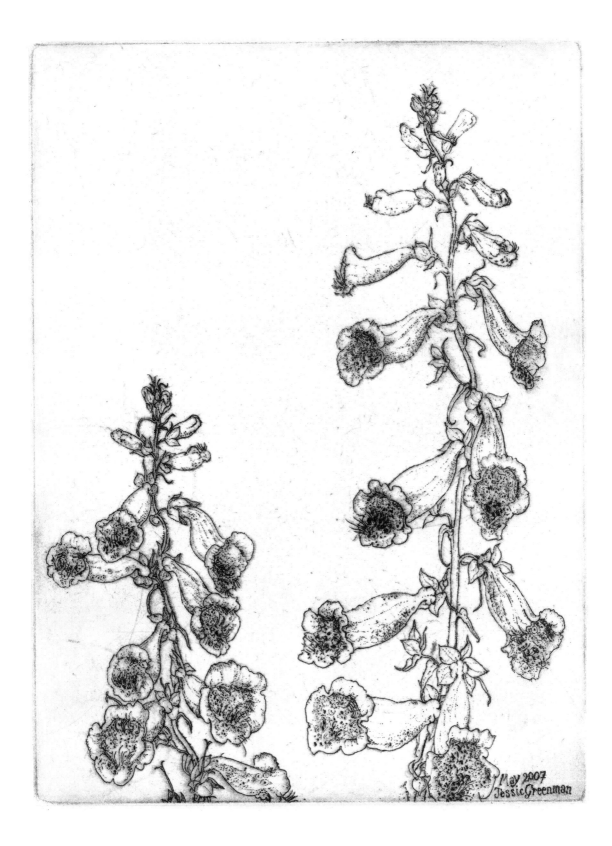

May 2007
Jessie Greenman

Narcissus

once I was half flower, half self,
that invisible self whose absence inhabits mirrors,
that invisible flower that is always inwardly
groping up through us, a kind of outswelling weakness,
yes once I was half frail, half glittering,
continually emerging from the store of the self itself,
always staring at rivers, always
nodding and leaning to one side, I came gloating up,
and for a while I was half skin half breath,
for a while I was neither one thing nor another,
a waterflame, a variable man-woman of the verges,
wearing the last self-image I was left with
before my strength went down down into darkness
for the best of the year and lies here crumpled
in a clot of sleep at the root of all nothings

Narcissus

Once I was half flower, half self,
That invisible self whose absence inhabits mirrors,
That invisible flower that is always inwardly
Groping up through us, a kind of outswelling weakness,
Yes once I was half frail, half glittering,
Continually emerging from the store of the self itself,
Alway staring at rivers, always
Nodding and leaning to one side, I came gloating up,
And for a while I was half skin half breath
For awhile I was neither one thing nor another,
A waterflame, a variable man-woman of the verges,
Wearing the last self-image I was left with
Before my strength went down down into darkness
For the best of the year and lies here crumpled
In a clot of sleep at the root of nothings
all

Alice Oswald

Lily of the Valley

A white-faced hanging-her-head
well-rooted woman used to live here.
Under the hips of the hills
in the arms of the valley.

Day after night after day
she stood here.
Hanging her head and letting fall her glances
on the tilted surface of the river.

Which was in fact the exact diameter
of the sphere of the valley.
The very tip of the cone
down which heaven was endlessly trickling.

And trees leaves stars everything
was always running down through stones
to this lowest level
of the lull between earth waves.

And hanging her head she said
I'm not leaving this valley
I'm going to bury my feet in the earth
they'll never shift me.

But they did.

Red-veined Dock

knock knock
knock knock
dear red-veined
liver-skinned
scalpel-trained
feeler of glands
with your soap-sweet hands
and warm glass wands
knock knock
knock knock
dear blood-stained Dock
it's me again
and I'm in pain
absolute eye-watering
voice-faltering
up-to-the-minute agony
which makes me scream constantly
can you hear me?
I need an appointment please
at every o'clock
let me in urgently frequently
you know it's me
with my dead foot
sore throat
demand for a sick note
and I know you
Dr Go-Slow
with your thick black eyebrow
and your bristly beard-shadow

I know I know
your noisy nose-blow
and the grimly to-fro
fetching of scissors
by your long fingers
and your sly certainty
that there is still no remedy
for mortality
except mortality

Fragile Glasswort

What can have happened to Fragile Glasswort?
She looked so controlled and thin in her green cotton skirt.
But she rushed out suddenly and was last seen in the marshes
standing in gumboots, weeping huge, mud-troubled splashes.

A build-up of salt in the gut. That's why she's so tearful.
That's why her gaze is as stiff and composed as a crystal,
till it frosts and dissolves. I don't know how to protect her.
I always knew from her brittle remarks she was likely to shatter.

But why does she not come back to discuss the whole business?
Certainly she is blessed with a certain hard softness.
Rigid but liquid. So very tense and splintery
you'd think she had a prong frozen into her of some ancient injury.

No true cohesion. That's what I always said.
I imagine she's out there still, sinking into the mud.
I'll go out later with a cup of tea and see if she's any less
fixed in her pressure and poise, internal and surface stress.

Narrow-lipped Helleborine

I'm worried about Helleborine. So hard-worked, so discreet.
So unhappy, so accepting, so reliable and so mute.
In her white nightdress, when she occasionally sleepwalks,
she resembles a closed umbrella, hunching her spokes.

She is to me much less open and spreading than she has been,
though sometimes, in a clipped, narrow-lipped tone,
she mentions work matters into a machine
and I can hear the dark shaft of her throat going down and down.

She speaks grey, as if under the shadow of some great regret
and yet will not say what and I know I know
there is a swallow's nest on the ledge of her window
that wakes her at four a.m., but she never says so.

Just glances and blinks and shivers and pimples
and sort of wipes the words away between mouthfuls.
She is to me much less talkative than she has been.
She looks tired in daylight. Almost green.

Pale Persicaria

In a ditch by the roadside,
full of sorrow sleepless,
under her breath, encouraging herself,
hands clasped in hope, long fingers.

No openings, no outlets in her eyes.
Lit dimly from within,
enclosed in longing.
It's dark in love. No sign. Still waiting.

White face. Green hair.
Blotched hands. No sign.
Little sigh hissing through pinhole lips.
Mouth readying itself for kissing.

Smoke-faint floating hope.
Impatient hope. Immense
lustless listless wishfulness
under her angle-poise heart.

Tingle of something opening close by.
Is it her eye?
She clamps her leaves to her
as if for warmth. And blinks.

Jessica Greenman 2008

Hairy Bittercress

Hairy Bittercress
ought to drink less.
She's so full of sadness.

You should hear her mutter,
her voice compressed by long thinking,
on her own all evening
in her TV loneliness.

'Blithering business!'

When she pulls off her tights
and sits with her white feet bare
and her legs a-prickle with hair.

What with swiping at flies
and a nasty word for the dog
and her ardent cindery shrew-small eyes,

all round her house
there's the fog and smell of old failure,
there's a dudness
fuzzing and shadowing round her.

'Blithering business!'

She sits so long
with that thought on her tongue,

sucking its bitterness slowly in
and stroking the tufts on her chin

and the way she weeps is so creepy-strong
in her tumbler of gin

ask her dog what went wrong.

Slender Rush

Too rushed,
too slender
is Slender Rush.

Prematurely wrinkled
pale hands
holding bags
hastily filled.

From the morning
to the evening
and back again.

Will she never
give up and sit down?

What?

Too morbidly
unblinking to answer,
too trembling and hurriedly
grumbling to herself.

Too off-hand,
too unwholesome is her manner.

Only bags of dried fruit,
improperly chewed
and digested en route,

are her intake. And for God's sake
where is she where on earth is she rushing?

Further and further
by waysides, heaths
and woodland tracts
growing thinner and thinner.

To her grave I suppose.
To her grave.

Jessica Greenman February 2007

Jessica Greenman April 2008

Interrupted Brome

Brome set out
to sweep the snowfall off his steps.
It was so cold. He had blue lips.

It was the darkest day,
as if the sun was an aspirin
being sucked away.

A dead crow fell whump on the mat.
When Brome looked up,
he found his foot stuck to the step.

'Help! Help! I can't loosen my fffft!'
The very words froze to a halt.
It was like banging at a rusty bolt.

At his wit's end,
with his tinfoil stare,
Ice-man, he stood shock-still there.

It took twelve hours.
Or was it years?
At last at last he limped indoors.

'Is that you, Brome?
You're back home.
I said you're back home.'

And so began an endless syndrome.
Now every time he speaks he pauses.
Halfway through a pause he freezes.

He starts to cough,
his eyes fill up with frozen tears.
And this can last for several hours.

Or is it years?

Mary Keen's Rambler

Blackberry

Clematis

Jessica Greenman November 2006

Rambling Rose

She could be any woman at all,
caught off-guard on-guard.
With her hands stroking or strangling and maybe
with her intentions half interred.
But she is as she is. Her foot is always
filing away at its cord.
And what she's really after
is to wander.

She forgets who she is.
She could be so small
she almost has no smell.
She feels like anyone at all.
When you walk up to her,
she keeps quite still,
but what she answers to
is never loud enough to know.

Eaten away by outwardness,
her eyes are empty.
They could be watching you
or not, they work indifferently
like lit-up glass and if you ask
why she won't speak, why should she?
When what she really wants
is to wander.

You know what women are like:
Sandra, Sabrina.

They pretend to be settled,
peering round under
the hoods of their names.
Alcestis, Clytemnestra.
She could be either of those.
She scarcely knows.

She goes on thinking something
just over your shoulder.
This could be the last day
before you lose her.
But what's the use
of saying one thing or another?
When what she's really after
is to wander.

Jessica Greenman 208

But what a beauty,
What a mighty power
Of patience kept
              intact
Is now in flower.

Snowdrop
Alice Oswald

Jessica Greenman February 2007

Snowdrop

A pale and pining girl, head bowed, heart gnawed,
whose figure nods and shivers in a shawl
of fine white wool, has suddenly appeared
in the damp woods, as mild and mute as snowfall.
She may not last. She has no strength at all,
but stoops and shakes as if she'd stood all night
on one bare foot, confiding with the moonlight.

One among several hundred clear-eyed ghosts
who get up in the cold and blink and turn
into these trembling emblems of night frosts,
she brings her burnt heart with her in an urn
of ashes, which she opens to re-mourn,
having no other outlet to express
her wild-flower sense of wounded gentleness.

Yes, she's no more now than a drop of snow
on a green stem – her name is now her calling.
Her mind is just a frozen melting glow
of water swollen to the point of falling,
which maybe has no meaning. There's no telling.
But what a beauty, what a mighty power
of patience kept intact is now in flower.

Jessica Greenman February 2007

Jessica Greenman Decemhember 2006

Mother of Thousands

Mother of Thousands
slaps the flour from her hands
and lies down flump in her loose-fitting stomach and elbows
in the arms of her warm old man.
'No rest for the wicked,' she sighs,
rolling a flan of sleep over her eyes.

Mother of Thousands of socks and toys:
she's a wasp in a tin
in her too small house, with its too much noise.
And she's pregnant again.
'No rest for the wicked,' she sighs,
rubbing the flour from her eyes.

Then it's hours by the bedside,
bored like an old old woman
riding alone on a bus
with her mouth dropped open.
'No rest for the wicked,' she sighs,
smelling the burning smell of her eyes.

A sudden updraught of dreams
lifts her away to a garden.
She's choking, she's coughing up sap
with her mouth full of pollen.
'No rest for the wicked,' she sighs,
opening the thousand flowers of her eyes.

Scarious Chickweed

Tap tap of approaching feet. Who's that?
Only himself, a little freakish man
escaping from the dark.
                    If he can.

Full length coat buttoned up to the chin.
Light shoes, very slightly stepped in.

His name is Scarious Chickweed.
He says so very quietly, very quietly indeed.
And sucks his peppermints very hurriedly, very hurriedly,
one after another after another after another.

Very small, shadow-lined face, short eyesight.
Comes to a road, looks left and right.
Stands there slumped, as if to hide his throat.

Hears a muttering sound, as of two murderers
whispering and sniggering.

            Who's that?

Only his hands, poor wilted hands,
winding and strangling a sweetwrapper
while he tremblingly stands.

Primrose

First of April – new born gentle.
Fleeting wakeful on a greenleaf cradle.
Second of April – eyes half open,
faint light moving under lids. Face hidden.
Third of April – bonny and blossoming
in a yellow dress that needs no fastening.
Fourth fifth sixth – she somehow stands
clutching for balance with both hands.

Seventh of April and tiredness shows.
No rest for three days in unwashed clothes.
Asks (eighth of April) for a little water.
Asks asks until the lips dry out. No answer.
Ninth of April. Head flopped over.
Contorted with headache. Seated figure.
Twelfth of April – eyes half closed.
No light moving under lids. Tense pose.

April the thirteenth. Almost dead.
Face like wet paper. Hanging yellow head.
Still there. Still dying. Fourteenth of April.
Face fading out. Expression dreadful.
Fifteenth sixteenth. So on so on.
Soul being siphoned off. Colour gone.
April the seventeenth. Dead. Probably.
Skull in the grass. Very light and crumbly.

Jessica Greenman April 2007

Procumbent Cinquefoil

That's that.
Flat on my face forever now.

The field
fully inhaled
and folded in its wings.

I'll tell you how it looks
without hope
at the groundfloor level of a hedgerow
lying staring at my handscape.

It looks endless.
A silvery bewilderness.

A carcass of stalks
through whose ribs the moon falls
like water
to the creeping base of everything.

And everyone is tall
and elsewhere.

Only my eyes are working,
waiting for a flower
to settle on my finger.

Yellow Iris

It's early morning
and a woman
from a previous
world is wading
up the stream.

Very stately and
sturdy with double-
jointed elbows she's
still in her
grave clothes,
her crinkled three-ply
surcoat made of
cloth of June.

She has one
gold-webbed glove,
one withered hand.

She's resting, considering
her next pose,
behind the blades
of slatted blinds.

Her name is
Iris, the Rainbow,
the messenger, the
water's secretary, the

only word she
speaks is 'yellow'.

Lost ghost Queen
of the Unbetween
it's lovely listening
to the burp
of mud as
she sinks her
feet right in.

Jessica Greenman May 02

Dense Silky Bent

Also there is an old man dressed in a rustling softness
with long washed hair and a little beard cut square,
often to be seen at dawn performing stretches to the sun
and doesn't care who watches, stares straight through anyone
with baleful, buzzard-on-a-fencepost vision.
When he leans to the side and breathes in loud and out
with accompanying swearwords, he seems small and sour
like a lost lover withered to a straw.
But when he forward-bends and his loose shirt
flops on his blinking eyes and swishes in the dirt,
sometimes we kick him from behind, he doesn't mind,
just springs up green again and stares at the sun.

Laertes. For Hamlet, and the trifling of his favour,
Hold it a fashion, and a toy in blood;
A violet in the youth of primy nature,
Forward, not permint, sweet, not lasting,
The perfume and suppliance of a minute;
No more.

Ophelia.   No more but so?

Laertes.   Think it no more.

Hamlet, William Shakespeare. Act I, scene iii

THE ARDE...   ...PEARE
AMIDS...   ...IGHT'S

Tessica Greenman June 2002.

Jessica Greenman
June 11th – July 2nd 2002

Poems

Etchings & drawings